Air

CONCEPT SCIENCE

Written by Colin Walker

Property of Anna Reynolds School

Air is a mixture of gases that nearly all living things need to breathe. The atmosphere that covers our earth's surface is made up of air.

The air in the atmosphere is thickest at the bottom. The higher we go, the less air there is.

2

At the top of mountains, there is not much air. Higher up, where planes fly, there is even less. Planes fly in this thin air to avoid clouds and mountain tops.

In space, there is no air at all.

Our weather is caused by warm air and cold air mixing. When warm air from the tropics meets cold air from the poles, they mix and we may get winds or clouds or rain.

Wind is moving air. We cannot see or smell air, but we can feel it when the wind blows.

When we run a race, we push our way through the air. The air moves to fill up the space behind us.

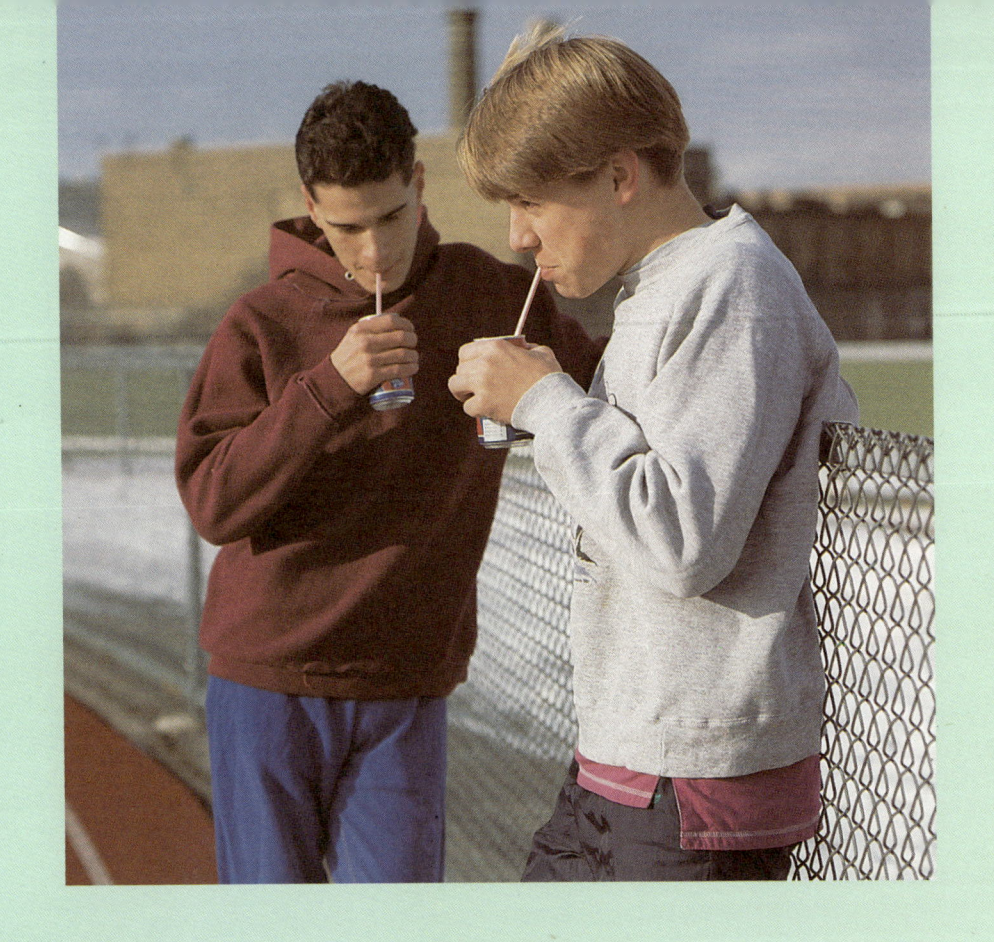

When we drink a can of juice after our race, air fills up the space in the can. An empty glass is full of air, even when it is upside down.

Air can be pushed down (compressed) so it takes up less space. Air is compressed in car and bicycle tires, and some machines also use compressed air.

Air presses in every direction. It presses upward, downward, and sideways on everything.

Try this experiment, using a full glass of water and a note card.

Even in water, there is air. If we cover a glass of water and leave it on a shelf for an hour, we can see the bubbles of air that were dissolved in the water.

Fish use this air to breathe. They take water in through their mouths, and their gills take out the oxygen in the dissolved air.

When we breathe in, air goes into our lungs. Our lungs take out the oxygen we need.

We breathe out carbon dioxide and the other gases from which air is made.

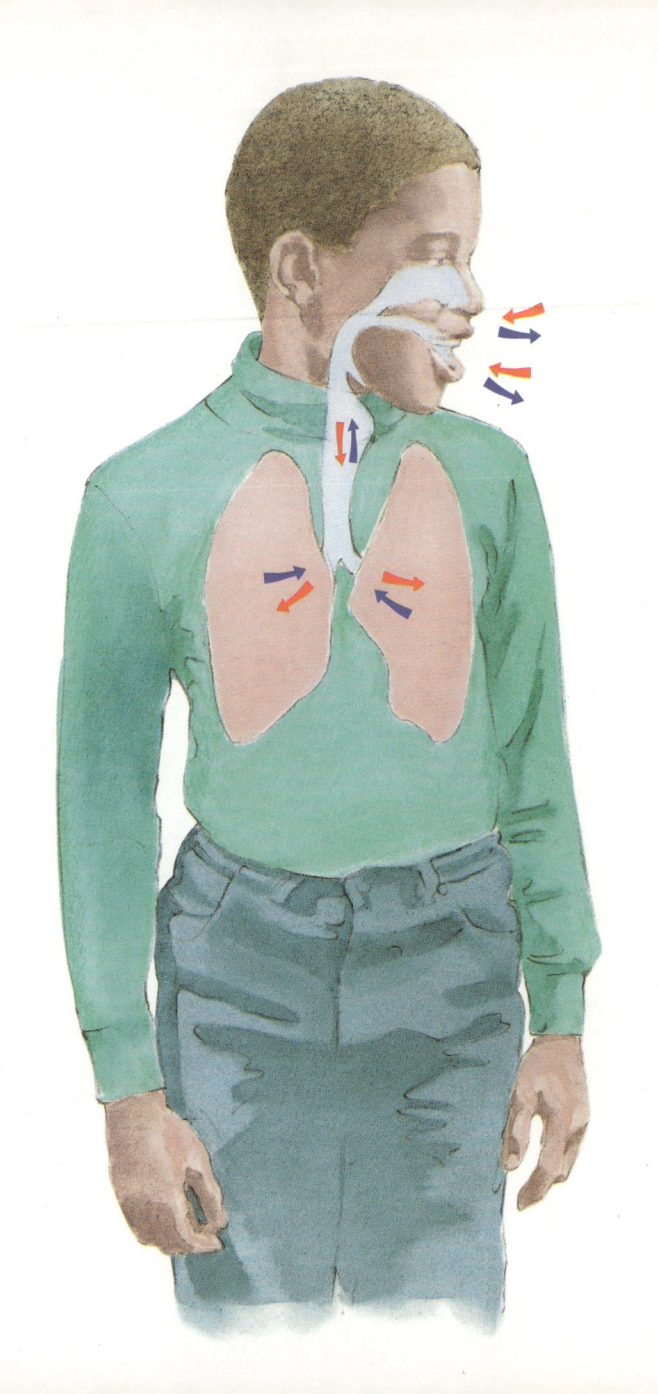

Plants take in air through tiny holes in their leaves. They use the carbon dioxide and give out oxygen and other gases.

Places that have no air, like the moon, have no animals or plants. Without the air in our atmosphere, there would be no life on Earth.

13

QUIZ

Where do we find air?

When a bottle of water is emptied, the space left by the water is filled up with _____ .

Can we see or smell air?

Moving air is called _____ .

When we breathe, we use _____ from the air, and make _____ .

Fish use their _____ to get oxygen.

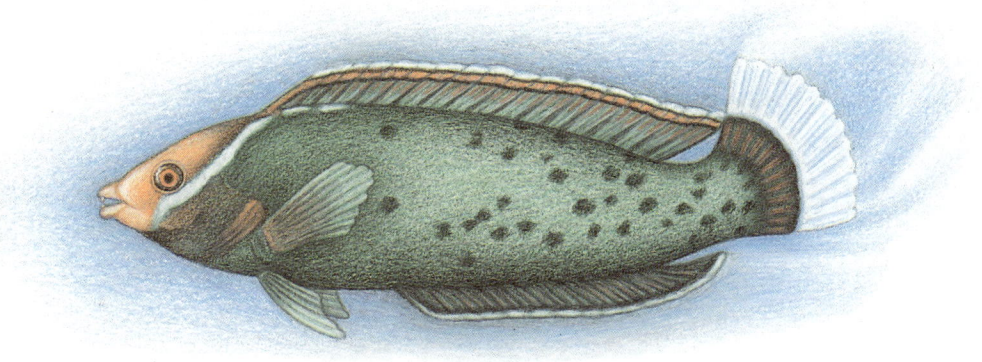

When plants breathe, they use _____ from the air, and make _____ .

Try these activities:

1. Imagine that you and your friends are going to live on the moon. You will take food, water, and other supplies, such as some air. What else can you take along to keep the oxygen in the air from being used up? Write a packing list for your move to the moon.

2. Put a drinking straw into a glass of water. Cover the top of the straw with your finger. Why does water stay in the straw when you lift it from the glass? What happens when you lift your finger from the top of the straw? Ask a friend to help you figure out why this happens.

3. Try pouring juice out of a can that has only one hole. Why does a second hole make the juice flow better? Ask an adult to help you find out.

4. Float a cork or a light piece of plastic in a bowl of water. Work with a friend to make the floating object sink, using a clear plastic glass.

[Here's a hint: The item floats in water because it weighs less than water. Does the object weigh more or less than air? Will it float in air?]

CONCEPT SCIENCE
Matter

Wood
Plastics
Air
Water
Glass
Metals

Air

Adapted from Concept Science,
© 1993, 1991 Nelson Price Milburn Ltd.
Text © 1993, 1991 Colin Walker
Illustration © 1993, 1992
Modern Curriculum Press, Inc.

MODERN CURRICULUM PRESS
13900 Prospect Road, Cleveland, Ohio 44136
Simon & Schuster • A Paramount Communications Company

All rights reserved. Printed in the United States of America. This book or parts thereof may not be reproduced in any form or mechanically stored in any retrieval system without written permission from the publisher.

2 3 4 5 6 7 8 9 10   96 95 94 93 92

ISBN 0-8136-7275-9

Printed on recycled paper